AND THEN I FADE TO RETURN

UMAR AWAIS

AURAQ
PUBLICATIONS

Printed in the Islamic Republic of Pakistan.

Printed: December, 2022
Edition: 1st
ISBN: 978-969-749-208-4
Price: Rs 1200 PKR, $12 US

AURAQ PUBLICATIONS

www.auraqpublications.com | raabta@auraqpublications.com
@AuraqPublications | @AuraqBooks | +92-300-0571-530
Printed and Bound by *Passive Printers* - www.passiveprinters.com

Table of Contents

Author's words:

Poetry, the word not only explains the expression through words but evokes the emotions, feelings, thoughts that one possessed in his/her mind and heart. I myself has expressed my feelings, emotions and love through words. Love for my family, friends and parents. This book contains all the emotions; happiness, loss, love and betrayal that everyone bears and struggled in his/her life.

Poetry is when an emotion has found its thought and the thought has found words.

(Robert Frost)

"Trees are poems the earth writes upon the sky, we fell

them down and turn them into paper,

That we may record our emptiness."

(Kahlil Gibran)

I wonder

I wonder what to write

With a cup of tea in a quiet night

With my eyes open to wide sky

Seeing starts shining bright,

My lips murmured, what a beautiful sight

Who is the one?

Who made this all?

This sun, moon and above all

These oceans, plants and all

Who is responsible for this magnificent call?

Why has He made this?

For us? Or for Himself?

Or just for fun?

Maybe there is a sign of things that run?

The time that runs, why doesn't it stop?

Who made this?

The time that never recalls

These questions asked by many

But the answer is same

And know, from where it came

The book who was sent by Him

From up the heaven that swims

A man amongst us was chosen by God

Blessed by a book and a perfect squad

Muhammad, was the name of the blessed man

Who was sent by God; and remember why he came

Spent his life in dark city

Turned people who were in pity

Being born orphan,

He was blessed by all

As he found Him, behind every wall

In the cave he listened His call

Read, O my love, read and recall

Recall my name who made all

You, sun, moon and all

And every other, even behind the wall

Being betrayed by people

He moved to the land, once cursed by evil

Spent day and night to teach all

The words he learnt from the one,

One above all

It says that love brings suffering

And their lives, start buffering

But as His concerns

He calls His man up in heavens and turn

Turned Himself to see him close

Stopped the time to learn him more

In His book he has addressed others

By their names, in numbers

But to address His lover

He speaks emotions, and

Hides him in cover

He called him when he was sixty-three

To offer him everything and to see him free

Humanity has never seen a man

More beautiful than him,

Or from where the life began

A sudden whisper

A sudden whisper in the air

Reminds me another glare

A glare that carries the sound

When the cold breeze blows around

A word winter that sounds strange

Yet everyone is ready to rearrange

To rearrange himself and his love

To create space for his beloved

Look! Winters are cold and dark

It tears the heart apart

Like every frozen thing

Comes the heart

Who knows how it will last

Look! The snow is coming down

Secure yourself

And your crown

Winter is coming

Coming like a stray hound

Stay...

Stay with me,

Yet another day

I still love you,

I still need you, don't go away

Stay...

Stay...

Because you want to

Not because I asked to

Stay...

If you feel okay

Stay...

Me, myself and 1

Look! It's me, myself and 1,

Who is waiting to die

Solo we come, solo we have to go

Everyone sees, and everyone knows

Far no one could hold your hands

There is only you, who stands

It's me, myself and 1, and to no one

I need to rely

Life is like seasons that change

Sometimes it's good, sometimes strange

I'm waiting, waiting for the end

I have no one...to whom I could depend

It's me, myself and I, and

I don't need anyone to whom I can rely on

Why is it that animals are bad?

These are humans who are mad

Mad at each other, and every other by

And at the end...who stays?

No one but...it's

Me, myself and I

A whisper

A sudden whisper without a sound

I hear while sitting on the ground

It was deep, and it made me bound

I saw everywhere, and there was nothing I found

Darkness covered my eyes, and I saw nothing around

With pain in my eyes, I drowned

Drowned with pain, and voices all over my head, and

It continued, continued to spread

I ran here and there for med, and

I felt nothing but hopelessness

Within me, I saw myself

Standing under a tree while holding my breath

I saw people dead, and

Vultures all over their head

Eating and enjoying their food

Some of the dead were crying, nude

I kept my hand on the bark

But it slipped, and I fell

I saw blood on my hand, and

It was coming, coming from where I stand

From the bark under the tree

There begins the blood, dripping free

My body starts vibrating with the tree

Like my soul was getting free

I saw myself in the swamp

Drowning under the dark bog

I hold my breath to be free, and

I was unable...unable to breathe

My skin turned blue, and it peeled off

I sat under...under the tree struggling, and I caught

As I heard the voices again, I called

Called my father, my God

He didn't hear, and he did not respond back

It made me sad

It happened again that I couldn't breathe, and

This time I freeze

I saw myself helpless, around

Suddenly, there appeared a hound

His red flaming eyes reminded me the death, and

He began eating my flesh

I cried...cried with pain,

For help but no one came

I saw myself crying in the bed, and

There was no one...

No one...in my head

Standing on the seashore

It was a gloomy night

With the bursting ocean in my eyes

I was standing on the seashore

Thinking about the love of a score

For heaven's sake, it was a swore

Staying together was kinda bore

With a glass of rum in my hands

And fire burning on the strands

I listened to the chirping of birds

Sitting on a cliff, off the shore

It reminded me of her allure

Her voice with a pleasing tone

Returning after my chore

I saw her sitting with another soul

She put her arm about his waist

And smiles like knowing her cake

Seeing this made me vexed, and

We had a son in the bed

He was in the home, playing alone

No one knew what could ensue

To see my boy, I made my quest

To my home, and leaving the rest

He was in the blood, struggling hard,

With a spur

Before I called for help, he was already dead

Ah, he was dead, dead

While lying on the bed

I was in shock, crying for my loss

For my son, no one was best, and now

He was at rest

After few hours, she finally arrives

And she didn't know the surprise

I asked her about the man

And she left our son, and she ran

Now he was gone, lying on the bed

Now you should go and leave for the best

She cried for forgiveness, and

I was sick of this tiredness

I asked her to leave, and closed

Doors when she turned her feet

She was crossing the road in sorrow

And was hit with a van, on the morrow

In one day, I lost my all

Knowing that it was my fall

Now standing on the seashore

Thinking what to say more

All this has happened to me

And yet God hasn't spoken for me!

O my life! My wish should be heard

I demand dead and leave the rest.

Sitting on the bench

Sitting on the bench

While having my lunch

Waiting for the train, while

Holding my coffee in the rain

As the cold breeze flows

It makes me love more

The drops of the rain kiss

The earth

And it seems that they were in love

Standing there and enjoying

The rain, I saw my train coming

It was raining cats and dogs

And the flowers seem to be

Dancing in the bross

I still remember the scene,

Ah! How it was pleasant and clean

It gave me pleasure and strength

To talk about the life that I went

You don't know how it goes, my dear!

Life is a mystery, which is not clear

Being born in the world,

It is not just only a curse

Think deep and find your ways

Remember your Creator and have faith

Our life is just at the extreme

Not knowing of what we have been

Complaining my luck

And this stupid being,

Where the hell have you been?

My life is there with no mean

The best and the worst,

I'm made to shuttle between two extremes

Oh, my love, where have you been?

I saw you struggling in my dream

You promised to stay with me

But you left me in extreme

Without you, I am lost

Thinking to end and take a pause

Who knows what will happen

My life will end in a second

My whole life is at stake

Time is running and is just a waste

Everything is clear and clean,

The best and worst, I'm made to shuttle between two Extremes

Now you're dead and

God knows the best!

The time will surely come

When we meet under the sun

The door of death is stopping my path

I will surely pass at any cost

I learnt that everyone here is mean, but
You should know life is just another dream

Life

Who knew what to hold?

Life is not a bed of rose

From birth till the death

We struggle hard till the end

Not knowing what is destined

We are merely at our best

So, what is life? A kite!

Flipping in the void

Not knowing what to avoid

Tied up with the string,

Flying around and round,

With a cling

With a loose string,

We are flying in the wind

Not knowing who we are,

We are indeed lost

With our eyes closed,

We are running behind our loss

Being thrown by the divine

Standing on the borderline

Living as a mortal being

Is a curse, and that's extreme,

Who knows the way it goes?

We are waiting for the day, of course

So, who are we? Why do we exist?

And if that's it, why do we resist?

Why do we die? Why can't we live?

Or do we have any free will? These

Are the questions that come again and again

But we know they can't be explained

Does He speak?

Does He speak?

Or listen to the words

Of those thirsty birds

Flying here and there

In search of water and

Waiting to be slaughter

Slaughter by fate or by life,

They even don't know

How to survive?

For they are disappointed by His grace,

Does he speak or listen?

Or they have to suffer their fate?

I listen, and I speak

You may not hear, But

You will see

When the time comes

You will see

For I listen to the words that you speak

Your thirst and hunger

It will grow younger and younger

For I the only one—I know

I know what is good and bad

So, you don't have to be sad

Time will come, and you will see

For I am the one who listens and speaks

The first time you looked at me

I know the feeling when

You first looked at me

I crumbled and twinkled like a star

Do you see the pain in my mind?

I was confused and didn't know what to define

Do you know the feeling? I tried to hide

I was shaking, and I cried

First time...

The first time you looked at me and smiled

I saw the ocean, versatile

The time stopped, and

I get copped

Copped in your elegance, and

There was no other relevance

Relevance, of your beauty

Your smile pierced my heart, and

It damaged every part

It cookout the darkness in me

The time when you first saw me

The time...

When you first saw me.

Can I call you?

Can I call you?

At my worst

There is ocean flowing, and

Is ready to burst

Can I call you?

When I feel thirst

Hope we can never be

Dispersed

Can I call you? When I am hurt

It's your thought

That helped me to divert

Can I call you? By your name!

I am lying on the floor, but you never came

Can I call you? On my death

You know it's my only breath

Can I call you? Can I call you now?

I was the one who was ready to bow

Can I call you? Can you listen to me now?

I will miss what we vow

Can I call you? Can I call you now?

You will be my first love

As you are now

Can I call you? Can I call you now?

Can I call you? If you allow?

Can I... Can I now...

If it's my last day

If it's my last day

Can we meet alone today?

My last...I want to spend with you

To feel like my life was also true

If it's my last day

Don't go away

Stay with me,

That's all I want to say

If it's my last day

I want to spend it with you anyway

To lay down on your lap, and

Take an eternal nap

I wish the time would stop

When we meet at last

If it's my last day

It will be mine anyway

People wished to fulfil their wishes, but

Look what I have to say

Holding your hand, till my end

That's it...what I want to say

If it's my last day

Let it be anyway

Remember me! My love

I will meet you above

If it's my last day

Let it be any way...

The love, moth and light

The power of the love

That remains

Listen to the words

That I want to explain

The love between moth and light

As the darkness wanted to be bright

Being born hideous and in dark

The moth was hatred by all

Being loved by her mother

He had dreams to cover

But as he belongs to the low class

He had to suffer a lot

Seeing the light and firefly in the school

He approached them as a fool

Witnessing the morning, he got lost

And he spoke so soft

The firefly kicked the moth

And he was down on the floor

With a torn cloth

Yet everyone smiled on his face

And he ran; he needed space

After some days, he saw her again on the wall

So bright, beautiful like a star

With sparkling tiny stars on her face

She made him enchanted in her divine grace

As he held her hand to touch her around

But he was hit by a stone, and he was on the ground

Father! Father! She called the sound

'I love him, and we are bound'

As he came to the house

Her mother held her child from the ground

And asked her not to go

Anywhere or another town

The light's father told her

That they had a class

And they and the moth

Had contrast

The light didn't listen to what he said

And she wanted her love instead

The moth left his house to her place

And they wanted society to accept their love instead

He was there, close to her to hold her hand

And everyone was witnessing their love to expand

But as he moved close to her to touch her around

He felt himself burning and drowned

The brightness burnt him alive

And their love struggled to stay alive

Seeing him dead on the ground

The light had a burst, a deadly wound

Everyone witnessed the lovers' death

Some of them held their breath

Leaving their parents speechless and bound

Both of them died around

The world says love is blind

And they don't support sometimes

For love sometimes is just a suffering

It feels like life is buffering

Why is it that the lovers have to

Suffer, or die?

Instead of splitting apart, can they ever unite?

And instead of being bound by the hounds,

Can they ever be crowned?

A Raindrop

I am a raindrop born in heaven

I feel like a burning canon

My parents are wind and cloud

We live in joint, and there's no doubt

I am in love, but she's not around

She is far, her name is ground (earth)

For every pain, there is gain

My love for her is not the same

For her love, and to meet

I jump from above to deep

There she is, expanding her hands

Welcoming her love to join hands

As I reach her place

I kiss her on her face

In her arm, in her hands

I give my life in the end

Friend

I know you are the one

Without you, there is no fun

When I feel low and find the end

I remember you, my friend!

There is one thing

That I must say

You need someone

With whom you want to stay

The one who could help you

In every way, and

Knows what your mind

Wanted to say

The one who could help you

In every way, and

Demands nothing

From you anyway

There are very few who stay

The rest of all is just fake

Always remember

The name who stay

They are the ones who remain

O' my friend, listen to the frame

There is dust and rain

But remember!

Always remain the same

Life and Death

Between life and death

There is a tug of war

Death is silent, and life snores

Imagine what will happen when they speak

Who is good, and who is creep?

Life said I gave hope

Hope to be reborn

Hope to cover slope

For death is dreadful, and what will she speak

She is dark, and she is a creep

Look toward my beauty and what I give

To the beings who want to live

They live the life and get what they want

What will you give?

Except for haunt

Death was there, silent and listening

She knew what she brings

To nature and the humans

What would happen

If I fall?

I know; I'm dark, I am creep

I'm dreadful; I'm deep

But listen!

Listen to my words, What I have to say

You! Dear life...is dreadful instead

I kill people at once

But you!

You kill them slowly and

Haunt

You betray them by showing the allure

Well...you are a killer, for sure

You are a lie; you brought suffering

Look at everyone!

How their life is buffering

Life is a curse, and yeah, it's worse

Listen! Listen to me and my every verse

Yes!

Yes, I am dreadful

But then, who are you a loose bull!

I would be writing about you

I would be writing about you, my love

You look as beautiful as a dove

For if there's live, the one above

May our life never shove

I would be writing about you for the rest of my life

Will you ever be my wife?

My love for you remains young

But our love...remains unsung

Blindfolded deception

Life: is it a newborn reality or a dying illusion?

It brings an ending without a conclusion

If life is a blindfolded deception,

Why can't we say anything if we have any objection?

Life: a blindfolded deception

Filled with many misconception

Struggling hard and hard like troop

It seems like we are caught in a time loop

Life brought nothing but pain

Working like angels without any gain

One day we will die; does it matter?

We die every day and every night

Steering in this blindfolded prime

Alone

Sitting alone near the muddy swamp

Thinking, how my life was chomp

Alone I was, alone I am

In the world like a little lamb

Like the phoenix, I burnt in flames

But I can't be reborn, what a shame

This means I am weak. Am I?

Or is it I who think deep

Why can't anyone understand

No one is perfect as planned

Alone we are, alone we will be

Without ourselves, no one could set us free

A Call to the wild, by the hound

(Inspiration)

These scars take the time

Look, I am stuck with the rhyme

Sitting in my house in the dark

Imagining, why are stars so far?

Besides the ticking of the clock

There was no sound in the dark

The sound of the void

Was terrified

With a page in my hand

I saw firefly in dark land

As it blinks and glows

It makes me think about those

From my window far to the ground

I saw eyes seeing me around

Those blue eyes, blue eyes!

We're burning like flames in the hedge

Seeing those eyes kept me bound

It seems like they wanted to say the sound

And I started to think around

Now the eyes are gone, gone!

With printed feet on the ground

Between trees, I hear the sound

A call to the wild,

By the hound

As I was sitting in my house

Seeing darkness above the ground

With a printed page on the table

And knowing, how does it sound?

Dried eyes

Look at those dried eyes

With no tears inside

Hoping to get what they want

Emotion lost in the storm

Look at those calm eyes

Pointing up at the sky

With hope or with the rope

They are broken from inside

Look at those crack hands

With no big demands

Look at those empty bellies

Empty, but still heavy

Heavy! But not with the food

With the hope to find no harm

And to regain the new charm

With the hope of better days

But how will they get and be praise?

Look at those tiny flies

Gathering on their face and eyes

With their children on the road

They don't have a home, of course

O' my Lord, help the poor

Humanity is so cruel

From their birth to the end

They are suffering, my friend!

She's changed

My love that remains, she changed

This morning I saw in her eyes

She's not the same

I could not feel what she obtained, and

Seeing her like this, I drained

As my soul has left my body

O she's changed

Maybe she will come...

Come back to explain

Or maybe she's not...she's not...

Thinking all in hollow, I strained

I fell for love

I fell for love in you

Yes...yes...it's true

I know you feel vulnerable

Yes! You made me too

From this time till the end

I will always be with you

Many hurdles will stop our path

Will you stay with me to go through?

Will you?

If I'm loved

If I'm loved by you

I would feel something new

If I'm loved by you

I could feel the way you

I know the past rests inside you

Will you love me? Will you ever do it?

I know the way you left me, and

It doesn't feel like something new

I'm crushed, I'm broken, and

I don't feel anything new

What if! What if I was loved,

By someone, but not like you

I am glad I met you

I am glad I met you

I am glad to say that

I am glad to see you

Hope you know that

I am glad I met you

I am glad you know that

I am glad I met you

I thank my Lord for that

The love always stays alive

The love you and I had

Was it fate or coincidence?

I am glad about that

If you love me, love me more

If you love me, love me more

Like it was never before

The love in me calls you...

Calls you for a reason, but

He thinks I'm in prison

That prison kept me away...

From you in such a way

That we are

On the same road by a different path

You rest in me

What rests inside me?

Is it you?

Or the one I know

The one who belongs to me

The one...

The one who truly knows me

The one, darkness I called

The one who I believed have died

Long ago...

Long ago when you left me

And you know...

He was the one who truly blessed me

I wished...

That it would be you

Who rest in me

I wished...

Martyr

There started a war, and

The enemy was not far

Before her son could leave the house

His mother kissed her young scout

While leaving, he held her hand

I think he clearly understand

Both hands were slipping from each other

He will be missing his mother

And there he was standing on the battlefield

Remembering her mother in the barren fields

He was wounded by the bullet in his chest

Lying on the ground, compressed

And there she was

With tears in her eyes

While remembering her only son,

She rise

His body was there, covered with mud,

For two days

Blushing under the sun

With a smiling face

She woke up from her sleep

After seeing her child drowning deep

She kissed the picture and hugged him around

Considering her son to be crowned

A sudden knock on her door

And she ran to hug her Thor

But there was no one

Except for some

Holding a coffin

In front of his mum

His body was there on the floor

It struck her inside, deep core

With a deep breath, she touches

Sitting beside him, she glitches

I'm the mother of Martyr, and I feel proud

He's not with me

But he's somewhere in the cloud

Waving me back and will remember my food

I'm the mother of Martyr, and

I feel proud

Come back

Come back and hold my hand

I am there...stand

Where you left and kept me wait

On our third date

Come back...and lay your hand on me

The feeling I love,

When you hold me

Since the birds departed

They left disparity for the trees

Come back...come to me

Hold my hand, and hold me

A call

Come to me, my dove

You are the one whom I loved

Why are you there, drowning in ignorance?

Why have you created such a difference?

You are me; I am you

My love for you always grew

So, come to me as I call

From God's heaven above all

You can't see me, and

I can't hear you,

But look! I am waiting for only you

Come to me, and hear my call

I'm waiting, waiting for you behind the wall

A new dawn

Silence everywhere, the silence around

The weather is blank as it sounds

There is no one, no one around

Listen to the darkness, how it sounds

Darkness is my toxic friend; it lifts, it settles

Here I am locked behind the metals

I spoke to the darkness, and it responded back

Darkness imposes itself like a rack

She is the one who stayed behind my back

It's been decades; I am away from my shack

Darkness in me, and darkness around

Look how they look profound

A hole inside the wall

From where the beam of light crawls

The darkness was broken by the light, and

It seems so much bright

Why a tiny beam has overthrown the darkness

I was overwhelmed by the hardness

But look! How the light is fading for breath

The darkness is giving her death

In the cabin behind the wall

I hear whispers and a call

A call of death, dull and depressed

Claiming her victory over the night

But it was just a beam in the night

Look how it shattered your throne

Think of when you will be alone

She will shatter and break your bones

Your darkness...

Your own darkness will make you blow

Night and Moon

Darkness that rests in me glitters around

Seeing my beauty, he drowned

How beautiful is the moon, and

Hides himself in the noon

We have children who glitter in the sky

Who gave pleasure to every eye

Look how beautiful is the moon,

When he is in boon

He is very moody, and he shows faces, but

I love him as he embraces

I feel unescorted when he's not around

He looked happy when I was around

I know

I know the way you love me

I know the way you miss me

I know the way you see

The path untrodden between us that flee

I know the way you kiss me

I know the way you miss me

I know the way you lie,

Listen...it makes me cry

I know the way how it feels

The pain and how it peels

The unlit darkness, and the cold numbness

It always makes a mess

I know the way you love me

I know the way you miss me

Don't leave me, don't die

You live in my eye

When you were going

When you were going

You didn't turn back

It hurts...

Like I was drowning in Fire

But you never came

For my sake or yours

You never came...

And one morning when I woke up

Your name didn't hurt

Maybe I was feeling free, but

I was happy

Happy...

When you were going

You didn't say goodbye

Goodbye...happy...

I was once loved

I was once loved, but

It was not you

It felt like something new

Someone close to me, and

That someone you knew,

You knew...

Once I was betrayed, and

It was you who made,

In me something new

I was loved, and

Didn't get hurt

Or maybe I was

But it didn't feel

Because I was desert

By you

I was...

I was once loved by you

Or maybe I was...

But it didn't last

Didn't...

Darkness

Darkness that rests around,

Listen to me!

I am already bound

Someone is resting in me

Already, and

He bears no pity

Look! Look at my city

How we hang around, and

Steady

There is no place for others around

So, don't knock on the door again

I have already someone found

Listen to the darkness that rests around

Silence speaks its sound

I have someone; I am already bound

What if!

What if...

What if I was loved by you, and

Maybe it would be true

What if...

What if we were never...

Never be separated and hated

Hated by the people

Around

What if the earth was profound

What if...

We were not born mortal, and

Seeing the world in rotten coral

What if...

What if we didn't fall from Eden

It makes us live with freedom

What if...

My wishes could be heard

I have spoken again and again to reword

What if...

What if...

The devil rests in you

Born superior, having pride

A man doesn't like anyone

By his side

The devil with evil's might

Is his friend and guide

Keeping away his life

He doesn't know what to decide

He was born with such pride, and

It let him divide, and

Now you are sitting like a bride

Waiting for the tables to turn by your side

The devil rests in you, and

You are occupied

Maybe it's the devil or

Maybe it's you... but you denied

The devil that rests in you

It's you! It's you! And yeah,

It seems right...

It seems right...

First time you looked at me

I know the feeling when you first looked at me

I crumbled and twinkled like a star

Did you see the panic in my mind?

I was confused and didn't know what to define

Do you know the feeling? I tried to hide

I was shaking, and I cried

First time you looked at me and smile

I saw the ocean, versatile

The time stopped

And I copped

Copped, in your elegance

And there was no other relevance

Relevance of your beauty

Your smile pierced my heart

And it damaged every part

It took out the darkness in me

The time when you first saw me

When you were going

When you were going

You didn't turn back

And it hurts...

Like I was drowning in Fire

But you never came

You never came...

And one morning, when I woke up

Your name didn't hurt

Maybe, I was feeling free

But I was happy,

Happy...

Have you?

Have you ever sacrificed your sleep,

Just to talk to someone?

Have you?

Look! Look at me, what I've become

Have you ever lost your friend?

Just to have someone

That someone you know, where is he?

Have you been able to touch one?

Have you?

The touch that causes a spell on the loved one

Have you ever lost just to be won?

Have you?

Have you ever felt like been abandoned?

And felt like you are none-none

Just like a body, whose soul has already run-run

Have you ever sacrificed yourself for someone?

Have you?

That someone close to you,

Where is he?

Have you ever...

Let's meet under the moonlight

On the 14th day of the moon

When it will be in full bloom

Let's meet...

Let's meet under the moonlight

During the night, at the hill sight

Let's meet...

With fingers slowly kissing each other

Sitting on the grassy shade

With my head on your lap, and

Your fingers playing with my hair

Let's meet...

Let's meet under the moonlight

When there will be silence around

Hearing our thoughts without sound

Let's meet...

Let's meet to see the love

Of the moon and the night

Look! The night holds the moon, and

Hugs her around

Let's meet...

Let's take a selfie

Look, it's first time we meet

Let's take a selfie or a memorial picture

Of you and me getting close

Enjoying the present and

Forgetting, how it will go?

Let's take a selfie with a different pose

O' I remember your every pout

I love the way you looked at me

Now let's take a picture

Of you and me

The memories that are saved with me

The childish pictures of you and me

It makes us close and even bound

Look! How we are profound

Let's take a selfie of you and me

Let's...

This isn't me

I think I lost myself

But I don't know where

Something is missing in me

This isn't me...

I don't know what to do

I want myself back as new

This isn't me as I grew

Maybe it's me, and I didn't know

But...this isn't me

Maybe the time has grew

Is it me? Or is it my view?

I think...

But this...

This isn't me

As I knew...

I call you for a reason

I call you for a reason

For I feel myself in treason

Last day when you left me

I can't feel myself within me

Come back, come to me

I am lacking myself within me

Hold on...listen to me...

You rest within me

I call you...

For a reason

Don't push me back in the darkness

It's calling me back, the darkness within me

I call you...

Call you for a reason...

Don't push in prison

By keeping me away from you

Like blocking the pollen from bees

Can I call you, please?

Look...here I am on my knees

My heart without is like a disease

I call you...

Call you for a reason...

Standing near the window

I was there standing...

Seeing drops of rain

Rushing downward in chain

I saw two drops struggling to move

All they wanted was to improve

Their to-and-fro motion kept me thinking

My emotion, my devotion

They were doing good,

Holding their hands to the ground

Like two beloveds were enjoying

Their foot in the mizzle

Suddenly, there came another drop

Creating hindrance in their path

Among one, he dissolved, and

Triggered the motion forth

The other drop left alone, and he saw her going

Like a bird clung into claws

Now he was left alone as I was

He was not moving forth

And there began the rise

He was standing there surprised

He saw his lover moving in front of his eyes

And there...right there...

He dried...
He died...

Look!

89

Look!

What I have to say

I want to say a lot of things,

But...

Never mind!

A cross verse desire

There was a time when I was mad for you

For your love and to see you every time

But look! Your thoughts are hindering me

To build a rhyme

There was a time when I was in love

And I gave everything to you, my dove

My time, my space, even myself

But you didn't care! Reacted blinded and deaf

I lost everything when you first said

Said the words that blew my head

I was happy that my love spread

But...I wasn't prepared for the thread

Now your trust and love are gone

But it's difficult for me to move on

I gave you everything you need

And you...only thought I am creep

What good I did, it does me wrong

And all alone every night, I wish so strong

I wish the world could turn upside down

And how I felt as alone in the town

I wish the world could turn upside down

And it will be your suffering, as

I suffered as a clown

I wish...

The world could turn upside down

And your smile could turn into a frown

I wish...

The world could turn upside down

And my darkness could cover you in a gown

I wish...

The world could turn upside down

And this time, it will be you as a clown

I wish...

I wish...

Colors

I'm black; I'm white

Why are we separated by the side?

We share the same parents

Then, why are we in a fight?

It doesn't matter who is superior or right

We are guided by only one light

Separated...yes, we are separated

Not by color, but with our twilight

We were born superior

But why do we judge others by colors

Black, brown or white, everyone is equal

In the supreme light

Be afraid of the flight

And there is no turning back from the height

It doesn't matter if she is black or white

One should have a beautiful sight

A trail

There is silence everywhere
And there is no sound in the air
Everyone is looking at each other
With their eyes hiding fear

Look! Who has been brought in the court?
Who is he?
Look! Who has been chained without support?
Who is he?

Who is he?
Who is suffering this pain?
Everyone is eager to know about
The man in chains

Look!
Look at him...his body is vibrating like
A beat of thunder in the sky
And there, he is standing in front of the high

Look! He is covered with a black veil

His hands are getting pale

Look at him...

Look! Who is he?

Soon, they uncovered the veil

And there it was...

An identity known as love

Love...who has failed...

Who has failed himself and others

Others...who were innocent lovers

This is the one who has killed a lot

Look! What has it brought?

Suffering...

Pain...

Weakness...

And stress...

Look! What he has brought

Who is he? A fraud!

Who is he?

Look at him! Standing like a dead soul

Lowering his eyes on the ground

Shame! Shame! Begins the sound

Look! Look at its face

Who has manipulated many with his grace

First man...

Firstborns...

And other folk tales around

He is the one who brought them pain

Pain without any gain

Look...at him

What a shame...

He is the one who has brought suffering and death

The high...looked at love

And there was no one, no one

Who could support him above

The high asked him to speak for himself

He was silent

Standing like a dumb

What could he speak?

He knows he is scum

(Love speaks)

There he spoke and broke the silence

Scum...who! Me?

I am not what you said

But it's the human who is dead

With a dead soul and dead body

Now, look! And listen!

I was made in heavens

And was buried in the heart

The heart of the mortal flesh

Pure I was...

Pure I am....

But I was led to be damned

By the people of the earth

With heart, nothing worth

Corrupted mind and corrupted soul

They were spoiled as a whole

I brought nothing but happiness

Pain...

Suffering...

I...I didn't dress

Tell me!

Who killed the first one on the ground?

They used me as a weapon,

To make it sound

I'm not responsible for the lover's sufferings

They have brought their own bringing

I was a blessing, not a curse

But they have made me...worse...and worse...

Bring the man in front of the high

A man shouted next to the high

A man was questioned by the high

Who speaks the truth, and who lies?

Who speaks the truth, and who lies?

Tell me!

Is it you who lie? Or you deny?

Who will speak for you? Tell us your reply

(Man speaks)

I speak for myself

And love spoke the truth, and there is no deny

But I was made pure

From the soil of Eden, pure

I was made as an embodiment of God

Considering me a liar seems so odd

I know I brought death and suffering

But listen! And see the bringing

Was it me? Did I commit?

Or the seven deadly sins of the pit

I was exploited, and I murdered my brother

Expelled from heavens, I suffered

I suffered a lot because of them

Lust...Gluttony...Greed...

Sloth...Wrath...Envy...Pride...

All of them...I suffered

I was pure...

But later manipulated by love and them

Is this my doing! O' I...

I condemn...I condemn...

(Seven deadly sins)

The seven deadly sins were brought in front of the high

They spoke that they would not lie

They spoke all in one

That we did not...we didn't do or done

It's their doings of love, and man

That brought misery to expand

And if we have done this...

But we haven't

And if we have done this...

We were not meant to do this

We were created to do this

Created by the humans...

Now, look! Look at him!

That little bag of flesh...

Is he destined?

Does his fate bind him?

He ate the fruit and was

Blessed with something...

Free will...Yeah, that's it

Free will...

Blessed? Said the human

Not blessed....

Cursed with that

And all this was because of you little hell rat

(High speaks)

Silence!!!

Said the high...

Who is it? That didn't lie

You all have manipulated yourself

And look what you have brought to thyself

Who is it?

Who has brought suffering and pain?

Is it love?

Is it human?

Or the hell...pain

Who is it?

Who...?

Words speak with words

Words speak with words

Yet, silence stays quiet and listens

Listens to the words, crumbled and loud

See that face whose lips are stitched

But his silence yet speaks of it

Why don't people speak?

When they found world creep

When their hands are tied up

Having the voice but didn't speak

You can't speak before the elder

But you see yourself dying deep

A man or a woman is kept bound

Why don't they have anyone surround

The world is a hell, entrapped in time

No one is allowed to speak; they think it's a crime

Silence is everywhere and it rules

In the world surrounded by fools

And there we are in the world of silence

Where everyone has voice, but stays silence

Look, it's love...pardon, the lost one

Silent...

And there's the honor, ah! respect

Silent...

Standing there laughing on man

Encaged in social boundaries

Seeing everything with his dead eyes

Listening the silence and how it snore

What is world? A hell to abhor

Silence is everything and it rules

Everyone is allowed to act like fools

The love

The love that blows

The winter when it snows

Every drop of rain that

Strikes the ground

It reminds me how beautiful

Does your name sound

Sitting on chair, holding a tea

Stirring with a spoon

And remembering, in my dreams

With every sip that I take

Makes me vulnerable and shake

Shakes me to the ground

The thought of holding your hand

How beautiful does it sound!!

April of 2022

It's April of 2022

These eyes remember only you

Watching you in the face of that shining star

It looks like the sky has a scar

A scar that seems wonderful

And attracts everyone from its pull

Look! Its April of 2022

And I only dreamed of you

Listen to my words as I must say

You're a scar who kept me astray

That bright face of you

It reminds me of something I knew

The one who appears in the sky

And her love never denies

Look! It's April of 2022

Listen to the words as you knew

I fell in love with a distant star

I fell in love with a distant star

The star which is way...far

I see it daily twinkling around

Sometimes in sky, sometimes on ground

Love, what it says?

An emotion, feel or just gaze

Look how I fell and had a scar

Love I cannot express; it's bizarre

Love, is it true as it sounds?

Sinking in pain, in a boggy ground

Yet, we love someone unknown

We tremble, rise to stay on ground

Sometimes all 1 think about is you

Sometimes all 1 think about is you

If I'm saying...listen, it's true

Sometimes all 1 think is to rescue

Rescue myself as 1 fall in love with you

Sometimes it felt like it will not peruse

Our love...as it's screwed

Can't make you happier now

As 1 once made a vow

Holding your hand in boon

Late night in the middle of June

Will it revive the lune?

And our dying fortune

Sometimes I think...

Think of you

Don't know how it ends

But one day it will renew

Someday, sometime all I think about is you

Only you

Trembling hands

Holding rice in trembling hands

I saw someone as dead land

Wrinkled hands, and wrinkled soul

She was dark as coal

With dried lips and white hairs

Her eyes were filled with tears

Standing near the leftover

She gathered her food, as she ate slower

With every bite she looked upside

Thanking God, or complaining the divide

Why He put bread in human hands?

Was He aware of the badlands?

He listens, He sees

But yet, He does not speak

He listens behind the shadows

The pain, suffering that overflows

He is the provider, and He decides

Then why is there a divide?

Divide it says, as it is human who decides

Who will live and who dies

May everyone eat well and thrive

For no one...

No one wishes to deprive

Every moon sight

With every moon sight

I remember your face bright

The white crescent that glows in dark

I remember every mark

Every mark on your face and soul

Which drives me crazy as whole

Remember! It's the start of July

When we said goodbye

Goodbye to the bad days

While holding your hand in a cafe

As waterdrops were kissing the ground

Holding your hand while having tea

It shivers me to the ground

Remember! With every moon sight

I remembered your name and write

A letter, a poem to keep us unite

And to remember you every day, every single night

Love the way you lie

I love the way you lie

And there is no deny

Love the way you hold

Your tears behind the cold

I love, even you said goodbye

Not only I mourn but this, this July

I still love and wanted to say bye

To hug someone and to die

Trembling hands

I wrote your name with my trembling hand

Sitting beside river on wet sand

Just as this river will our love ever expand

Tears in my eyes and painful gland

I wrote,

Wrote your name with my trembling hand

Look! Look at the river how it covers sand

Erased your name, as planned

What's love? Is it planned?

You cry, you weep, you demand, and you stand

Encaged in boundaries or get banned

What is love?

Did you understand?

2 a.m.

2 a.m. in the night

Seeing moon shining bright

With my leg on my thigh

Pushing my thoughts, and saying them, Hi!

Bursting thoughts and trembling hands

Tears in eyes with painful glands

I see myself stuck and high

Drowned in sea in dark blue sky

Encaged with problems and handcuff tight

Is it family, friends or just earthly lie?

Seeing myself weak and shy

I remember myself weak, saying Hi!

Being stuck here and there, I hear a bell

My phone rings and casts a spell

Seeing it will be okay! A text

I forget all my worries

At best...

At best...

Printed and Bound by *Passive Printers* - www.passiveprinters.com
Printing press that offers Print on Demand (POD) Facility.
Printed in The Islamic Republic of Pakistan.